W9-BIE-309

Animal Attraction

Inside the Beastly Singles Scene

Hylas Publishing®
129 Main Street, Ste. C
Irvington, NY 10533
www.hylaspublishing.com

Copyright © 2008 by Hylas Publishing®
Used under license. All rights reserved. The moral right of the author has been asserted.

Hylas and the Hylas logo are trademarks of Hylas Publishing, LLC.

All rights reserved under International and Pan-American Copyright Conventions. No part of this publication may be reproduced, stored in a retrieval system, or transmitted in any form or by any means, electronic, mechanical, photocopying, recording or otherwise, without the prior written consent of the copyright holder.

Hylas Publishing
Publisher: Sean Moore
Art Director: Gus Yoo
Editorial Director: Ward Calhoun
Photo Editor: Ben DeWalt

ISBN-13: 978-1-4351-1021-2

Printed and bound in China

First American Edition published in 2008
2 4 6 8 10 9 7 5 3 1

Animal Attraction

Inside the Beastly Singles Scene

WARD CALHOUN

Tell me, exactly when did we become one of those obnoxious couples who dress alike?

I think three days of foreplay is enough already.

Get a room!

"That's why the lady is a tramp."

What do you mean you can't find it? I've never been so insulted!

Well, that was certainly fast. But I guess I shouldn't be surprised.

What happened to us? We used to be such swingers.

All this for a salmon dinner . . . I'm such a slut!

I don't mind telling you, this foot fetish of yours is a little weird.

You know, for a thoroughbred, you're not very thorough.

Men are such pigs.

You're grrrrrrreat!

I can't believe I can't remember where I parked the car. She's never gonna let me forget this.

Hey, I'm all for a little kink, but these golden showers are giving me one in my neck.

I'm old and horny . . . so sue me.

Another kiss on the cheek? Jeez, how many checks does a guy have to pick up?

Your name is Dolly?
Seriously?
That's hysterical.

Eh, you're not so smart. I convinced you to sleep with me on the first date, didn't I?

Here comes
Peter Cottontail.

You know you've been home on the range way too long when *that* starts looking good to you.

When you said you were going to share your nuts with me, this is not what I had in mind.

I'm sorry I haven't called—I've been swamped.

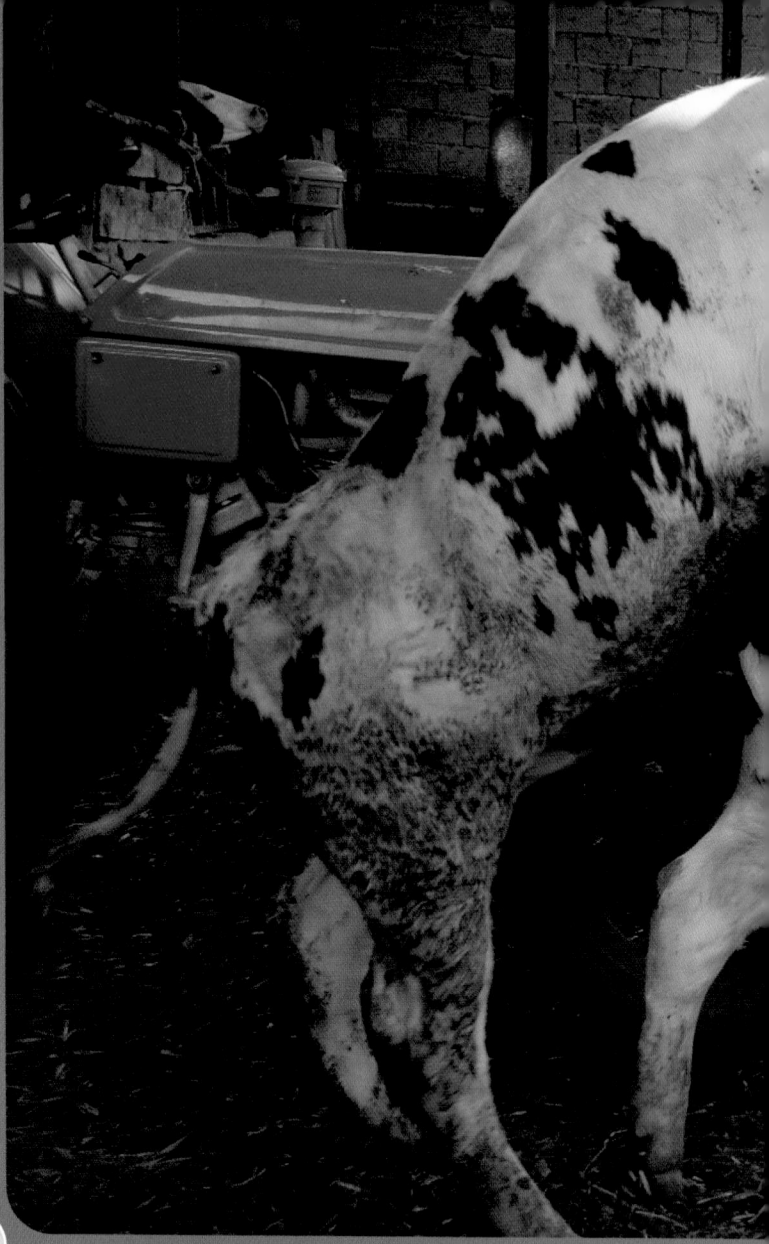

Did you just say boo?
Are you booing me? I mean
I'm doing my best here and ...
Excuse me? Moo?
Oh ... um ... never mind.

Where's the zipper on this thing?

Boy, you sure are one horny toad.

So, do blondes really have more fun?

You almost finished?

In a while crocodile.

Sheesh! I specifically told the dating service not to set me up with any more dogs.

Sigh—
another shrimp on
the Barbie.

Aw, not again!
I'm gonna start calling
you the polar express.

No, really, when it's not cold it's *this* big!

Well, I guess you just answered the "which came first?" question.

I gnu you couldn't stay mad at me ...

Our love life has really improved ever since he started taking Flyagra.

I'm sorry, I'm sure you're very nice, but things are moving much too fast for me.

I'm all for swinging, but this is a little bananas.

For the last time, *yes* I took the trash out. Now will you please get off my back already?

So we're in agreement, oral sex is out of the question.

This is more like a 67, not a 69.

Iguana make
love to you.

I've got to say, I've been on some crappy dates before but this takes the cake.

Cattle drive?
I got your cattle drive right here.

Someone's been eating out of the trash can again.

You're not coming anywhere near me until you shave those whiskers, mister.

Just keep those flippers where I can see them, buddy.

Ugh, get off of me,
You are so fowl.

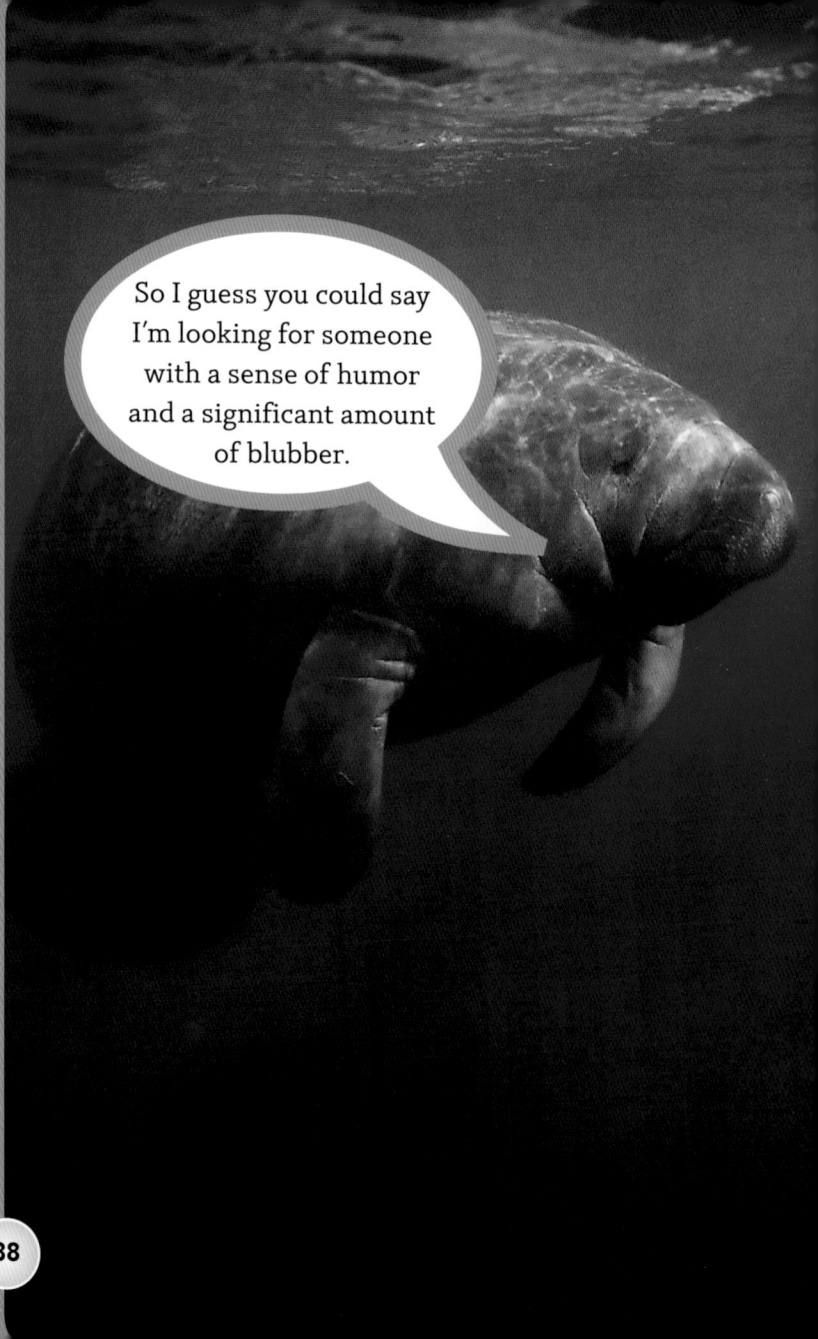
So I guess you could say I'm looking for someone with a sense of humor and a significant amount of blubber.

Faster, Henry! Faster!

I'm sorry my place is such a sty.

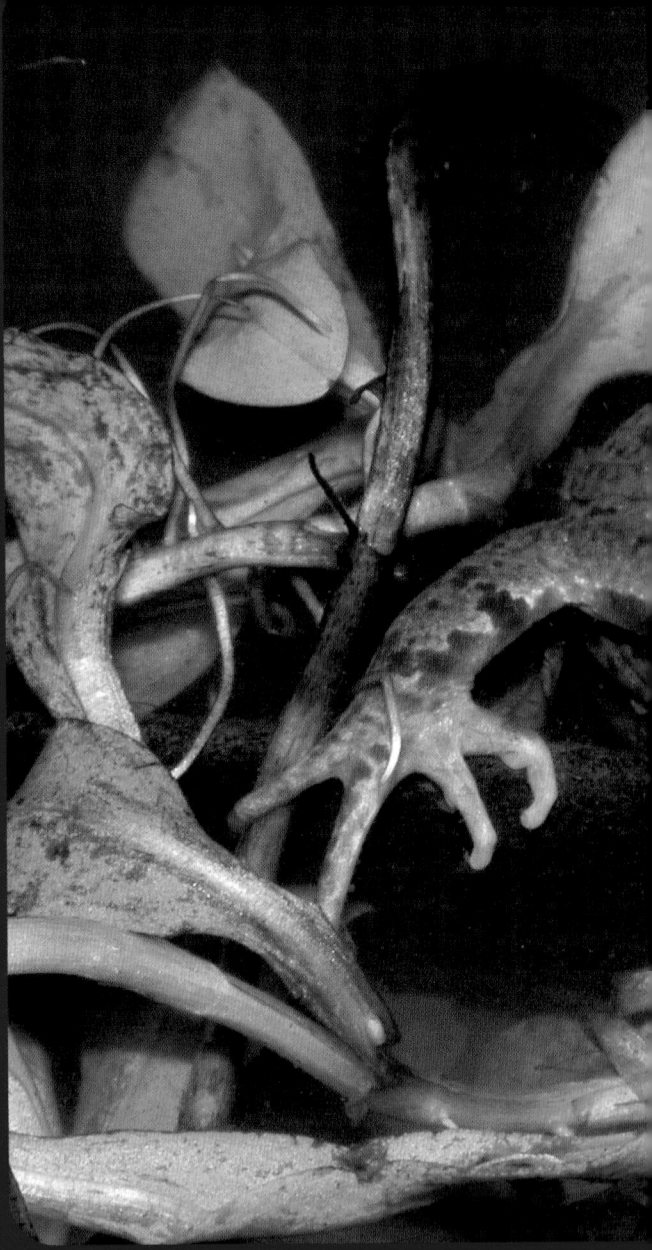

I know this isn't the most romantic spot, but my pad's a mess and full of flies.

Is she asleep yet?
I mean, how much longer
do I have to cuddle?

I like the girls with the junk in the trunk.

What am I doing with this old buzzard?

Listen, no offense, but your sexual technique is strictly for the birds.

You think just because I have a slight "odor problem" that I'll go out with just anyone?

Baby got back.

So, your shell or mine?

I just said I wanted to go south. Why are you freaking out?

Who said wasps don't have great sex?

To be honest, Percy, I really don't give a hoot about you.

I find that a little grass really helps me to relax, don't you?

I wish you'd stop referring to me as your old bag. You know half of my family ended up as luggage.

It's good
to be the king!

Nice rack!
Are they real?

Oh yes! This is better than a whole bucket of fish! Give it to me, baby!

This sure beats sitting on a pile of dog crap.

I hope this guy doesn't give me crabs.

Photography Credits

4–5: Photos.com/© 2007 Jupiterimages Corporation; **6–7:** ShutterStock/Paul Topp; **8–9:** Animal Attitude CD; **10–11:** ShutterStock/Steve McWilliam; **12–13:** Photos.com/© 2007 Jupiterimages Corporation; **14–15:** Photos.com/© 2006 Jupiterimages Corporation; **16–17:** Photos.com/© 2007 Jupiterimages Corporation; **18–19:** ShutterStock/Richard C. Bennett; **20–21:** Index Open/FogStock LLC; **22–23:** ShutterStock/Nick Stubbs; **24–25:** Photos.com/© 2007 Jupiterimages Corporation; **26–27:** ShutterStock/William George Hagerbaumer; **28–29:** Photos.com/© 2007 Jupiterimages Corporation; **30–31:** iStock Photo/Rob Friedman; **32–33:** Photos.com/© 2007 Jupiterimages Corporation; **34–35:** Index Open; **36–37:** ShutterStock/Nicholas Raymond; **38–39:** Photos.com/© 2007 Jupiterimages Corporation; **40–41:** ShutterStock/aaaah!; **42–43:** Photos.com/© 2007 Jupiterimages Corporation; **44–45:** iStock Photo/Steve Geer; **46–47:** Photos.com/© 2007 Jupiterimages Corporation; **48–49:** iStock Photo/Dragan Trifunovic; **50–51:** Index Open/photolibrary.com pty. ltd.; **52–53:** ShutterStock/SF Photography; **54–55:** ShutterStock/Elisa Locci; **56–57:** ShutterStock/Stuart Elflett; **58–59:** Animal Attitude CD; **60–61:** ShutterStock/Andy Lim; **62–63:** Big Stock Photo/Wallbanger; **64:** Photos.com/© 2007 Jupiterimages Corporation; **65:** Index Open/FogStock LLC; **66:** Photos.com/© 2006 Jupiterimages Corporation; **67:** ShutterStock/Raymond Lin Wenwei; **68–69:** Photos.com/© 2007 Jupiterimages Corporation; **70–71:** Photos.com/© 2006 Jupiterimages Corporation; **72–73:** Photos.com/© 2007 Jupiterimages Corporation; **74–75:** Photos.com/© 2006 Jupiterimages Corporation; **76–77:** Index Open; **78–79:** ShutterStock/Rebecca Picard; **80–81:** Photos.com/© 2007 Jupiterimages Corporation; **82:** ShutterStock/PMLD; **83:** Photos.com/© 2006 Jupiterimages Corporation; **84:** Index Open; **85:** Photos.com/© 2007 Jupiterimages Corporation; **86–87:** ShutterStock/Andre Nantel; **88–89:** Index Open/Frank Staub; **90–91:** ShutterStock/Alistair Cotton; **92–93:** IndexOpen/Photos.com Select; **94–95:** ShutterStock/Steve McWilliam; **96–97:** Photos.com/© 2007 Jupiterimages Corporation; **98–99:** ShutterStock/Chris Fourie; **100–101:** Photos.com/© 2007 Jupiterimages Corporation; **102–103:** ShutterStock/J_S; **104:** ShutterStock/Holly Kuchera; **105:** Photos.com/© 2007 Jupiterimages Corporation; **106–107:** ShutterStock/Sarah Jo Ochoa; **108–109:** Index Open/Keith Levit Photography; **110–111:** Photos.com/© 2006 Jupiterimages Corporation; **112–113:** Index Open; **114–115:** Photos.com/© 2006 Jupiterimages Corporation; **116–117:** Photos.com/© 2007 Jupiterimages Corporation; **118–119:** Index Open/Fogstock LLC; **120–121:** Index Open; **122–123:** ShutterStock/Foxie; **124–125:** ShutterStock/Tan Hung Meng; **126–127:** Big Stock Photo

Acknowledgments

The author would like to thank his wife Kimberly for being kind to dumb animals such as himself. This project also benefited greatly from the work of design dynamo Gus Yoo and editorial whiz kid Rachael Lanicci. Finally, special thanks to Ben DeWalt and Matthew Gross for their caption contributions.